The Romantic Spirit 1790–1910

Selected, edited and annotated by Nancy Bachus

23 Early Intermediate to Intermediate Piano Solos
Reflecting 19th Century Society, Style and Musical Trends

Cover art: *Frédéric Chopin in the Salon of the Prince Anton Radziwill*
by Henryk Siemiradzki (1843–1902)
AKG Photo, London

*F*oreword by Fernando Laires

Nancy Bachus's *The Romantic Spirit* is brilliantly conceived for both the present and the future. The new century will inevitably bring new ways of life and educational values that will challenge piano teachers to reevaluate the purposes and orientation of their teaching. While music will remain essential to human beings and to the education of the young, new teaching ideas will be needed to adapt to the future dynamics of our changing society.

Illustrated with historical paintings and quotations, and containing information about composers, the style of their works and the mechanism of the piano, *The Romantic Spirit* meets this challenge by showing students music's relationship with literary, scientific, social and political events. This integration of music with other fields of knowledge broadens the scope of their education, and promotes greater interest in continuing piano studies.

The pieces are of contrasting moods, tempos, forms, styles and piano techniques. The music is sure to spark students' interest as the pieces are engaging to learn and perform. Because of the special educational value of *The Romantic Spirit* and also because it is advisable for students to learn works above and below their current level, the music in *The Romantic Spirit*, Books 1 and 2 may be studied in any order.

The Romantic Spirit is certain to be an indispensable resource for every piano teacher and student.

*F*ernando Laires *has successfully combined an international career as concert pianist, recording artist and teacher. For his debut in Lisbon, Portugal, at age 19, he performed all 32 Beethoven piano sonatas in a series of 10 recitals. Mr. Laires has held artist faculty positions at various institutions in Europe, the United States and in China. He is co-founder and current president of the American Liszt Society. In addition, he has served on the juries of many international piano competitions, including the Tchaikovsky in Moscow and the Van Cliburn in Texas.*

*P*reface by Nancy Bachus

To understand and interpret musical style one must recapture the spirit of the environment in which composers lived, created and performed. Romantic music developed in 19th-century Europe when musicians were frequently writers, painters, philosophers and historians as well as masters of their musical art. *The Romantic Spirit* comes alive by integrating historical information and artwork with the piano pieces written during this period. Knowledge of the great attainments and heritage of our Western civilization fosters a deeper and more personal lifelong experience with the great art of piano playing.

*N*ancy Bachus *is a graduate of the Eastman School of Music where she studied with pianist Eugene List and accompanist Brooks Smith. Her articles have been published in various keyboard magazines. Nancy has taught over 25 years at the college and university levels as well as at the National Music Camp at Interlochen, Michigan. Certified as a Master Teacher by the Music Teachers National Association (MTNA), Nancy currently maintains an independent piano studio in Hudson, Ohio. A teacher and recitalist, she has been a featured clinician for numerous piano teachers' organizations and music conventions.*

Contents

usical Style

Musical style comes through musicians as a result of their individual personalities and the characteristics of the times in which they live. Musical style differs according to:

- **who** composed the music.
- **where** it was written.
- **when** it was written.
- **why** it was written.

omantic Style Period (1790–1910)

Giusseppe Verdi conducting.

The name for the **Romantic Period** came from literature. A romance (*romans*):

- referred originally to writings in one of the Romance languages (languages that were derived from Latin).
- is a fictitious poem or tale, written imaginatively.
- is subjective, written from the personal viewpoint of the artist.
- is often set in nature (such as a forest or an exotic far-off country).
- is usually about a heroic person or event involving adventure, love or the supernatural.
- is associated with something far away, strange, imaginative or full of wonder.

The Romantic Period was a time of great change in:

- the way countries were governed.
- the way individuals worked, lived and used their leisure time.

Political Changes: The French and American Revolutions

Political changes were brought about by events in the late 1700s, such as the French and American Revolutions. During this time:

- individuals overthrew governments of kings and queens.
- newly formed governments allowed people to elect their own political leaders.
- the idea that all people should be equal and free to rise from a low position to one of prominence and power through personal effort began to gain acceptance.

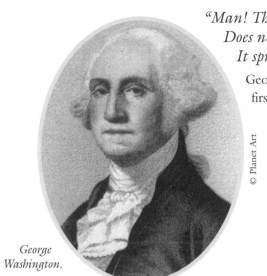

George Washington.

"Man! Thy merit upon the earth
Does not depend upon thy birth;
It springs from character alone."
George Washington (1732–1799),
first President of the United States.[1]

A life without stain, a fame without flaw.
William Makepeace Thackeray (1811–1863),
British novelist, on Washington[2]

He is next only to the divinity.
Lord Byron (1788–1824),
English poet, on Washington[3]

Social Changes in the 19th Century

Threshing machine.

The Industrial Revolution

The **Industrial Revolution** was a time when hand tools were replaced by power tools and machines, changing the lives of individuals.

- Mechanical inventions and labor-saving devices, such as the cotton gin (1791), machines for steel production, electric lights, food canning and office machines, made people's lives easier.

Increased scientific knowledge also brought about changes through:

- improved transportation with the steam boat (1802) and railroad (1825).

- improved communication by telegraph (1832), photography (1839), undersea telegraph cables (1866), telephones (1876) and phonographs (1877).

Early phonograph.

- greater knowledge of medicine and sanitation, which helped control many diseases.

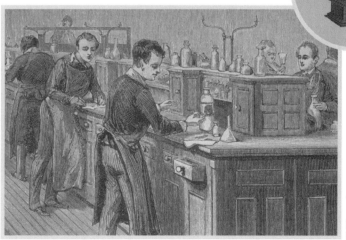

Scientific reseach.

[1] J. Barzun, ed., *The Pleasures of Music* (New York: Viking Press, 1951), 233.

[2] Roger Bruns, *George Washington* (New York: Chelsea House, 1987), 107.

[3] Ibid., 103.

Musical Life

With machines doing work previously done by hand, people had more leisure time, and used it:

- to study music themselves.

- to attend public concerts in the newly constructed theaters and halls.

With more people being exposed to music, the demand for music brought about new music-related businesses and industries, such as:

- music conservatories or schools, which developed in most major cities to meet the increased need for performers and teachers.

- an increased number of manufacturers of pianos and other musical instruments.

- concert societies and promotional agencies.

- music publishing.

Barbershop quartet.

In earlier times, concerts were usually held in palaces or large cathedrals, since most music was written for royalty or for the church. In the 19th century,

- with improved transportation and new concert halls, more musicians made careers of touring and performing.

- composers and performers frequently arranged concerts at their own expense to become known and to earn money.

Piano advertisement.

Romantic Ideals

Romantics searched inside themselves to find deeper meaning to life. Romantics had many beliefs:

- The primary purpose of art was not to serve or amuse royalty (which was the classic ideal).

- Each artist had the freedom to express intimate personal feelings through his or her art.

- Artists expressed deep and noble thoughts, their individual beliefs and their moods through their art.

- Poets and artists were heroes and could help society by finding high, uplifting values in life.

- The world was best understood by using emotions and feelings, not intellect and reason.

- Imagination and the fantastic should be used to move and impress people.

Corbis-Bettmann

This engraving of Lord Byron (1788–1824), the English poet, illustrates the Romantic point of view:

- The artist has withdrawn from public life and society.

- Being alone, the artist can better release creative energy.

- Living in nature, the artist will have greater spiritual insight.

- The society that most interests the artist is from the past.

- Great and noble traditions of that society are now in ruin.

Transition: From Classical Style to Romantic Style

Ludwig van Beethoven (1770–1827) is known as a **Classical-Romantic** composer.

- His music is a bridge between the two periods.

- He performed for Wolfgang Amadeus Mozart (1756–1791) when he was young.

- He studied composition with Franz Joseph Haydn (1732–1809).

His life was that of a true Romantic artist.

- He had great personal suffering.

- He became deaf at the height of his fame as a pianist.

- He then isolated himself from others.

- He lived only for the art of music and the good it could do for mankind.

"I shall seize fate by the throat; it shall certainly never overcome me."
Beethoven[4]

Beethoven in his studio.

AKG London.

© Planet Art

[4]Letter to Freiherr Zmeskall von Domanowecz, 1798, *Dictionary of Musical Quotations*, Derek Watson, ed. introduction and selection (Ware Hertfordshire: Cumberland House, Wordsworth Editions Ltd., 1994), 113.

Beethoven is best known for his monumental 32 sonatas for piano, but he also wrote three sets of pieces he called *Bagatelles.* Bagatelle is French for "trifle," or a short piece.

Bagatelle

Ludwig van Beethoven (1770–1827)
Op. 119, No. 9

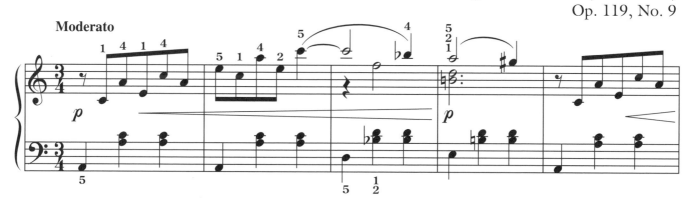

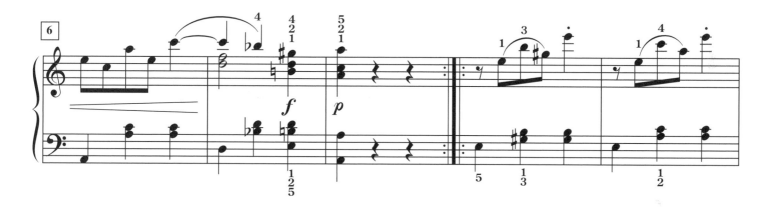

The Piano: Instrument of the Romantic Period

The piano became a musical symbol of the Romantic spirit of individualism and freedom:

- It could be played by one person.

- It had a dynamic range from a whisper to overpowering thunder to convey a wide range of feelings and emotions.

- It could be used at home, in a salon or on a concert stage for personal expression.

- The Industrial Revolution, with its factories, mechanical improvements and improved manufacturing processes, made pianos available and affordable to many people.

Ignaz Joseph Pleyel (1757–1831) began making pianos in Paris, France in 1807. These pianos:

- became the main rival to the Érard piano (at that time, the leading French piano).

- were the pianos Frédéric François Chopin (1810–1849) felt were the most suitable to convey his own special "singing" tone.

Pleyel's piano factory (below) and his upright piano (right), 19th-century Paris.

The Aristocratic Minuet

The **minuet** was a dance form that began in the Baroque Period and remained popular throughout the Classical Period. It was:

- one of the most popular social dances of European aristocratic society from 1650–1800.

- dignified, because balance and control were required to dance the very small steps.

- a moderately slow, elegant, graceful dance in triple meter (usually in $\frac{3}{4}$ time but sometimes in $\frac{3}{8}$ or $\frac{6}{8}$ time).

- two measures long in the basic dance unit, giving an accent every six beats.

- originally two eight-measure phrases, with each phrase usually repeated.

- made longer by adding a second minuet (known today as a trio). The trio had a different feeling or mood, with a contrast in key and thematic material. Second minuets were usually written in three-part harmony.

Examples of late 18th-century aristocratic clothing styles.

President George Washington dancing a minuet at his Inaugural Ball in 1789.

Ignaz Joseph Pleyel studied composition with Franz Joseph Haydn (1732–1809), and his music was praised by Wolfgang Amadeus Mozart (1756–1791). In addition to being a piano manufacturer and composer, Pleyel was also a conductor, music seller and publisher.

Minuet in C Major

Ignaz Joseph Pleyel
(1757–1831)

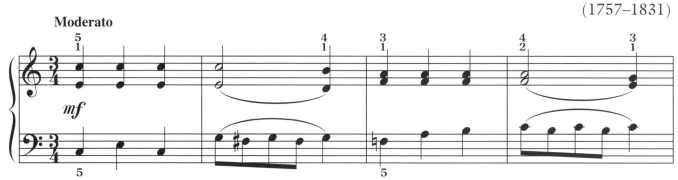

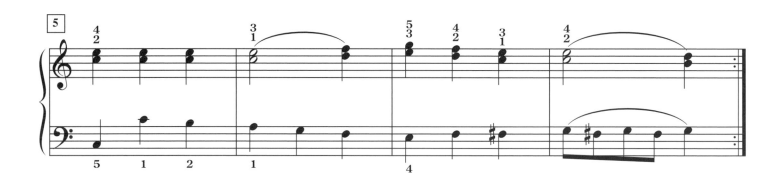

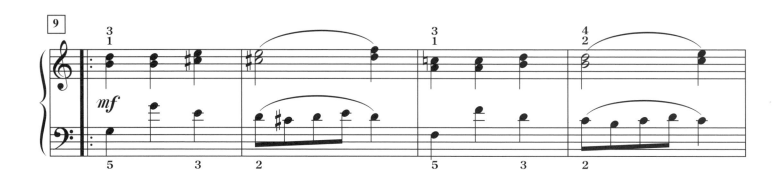

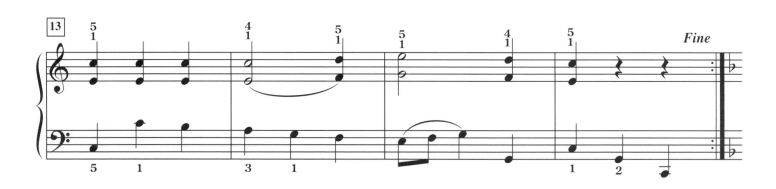

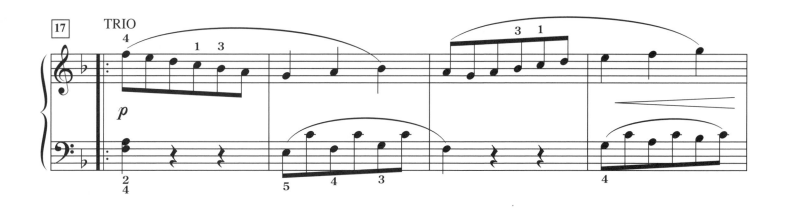

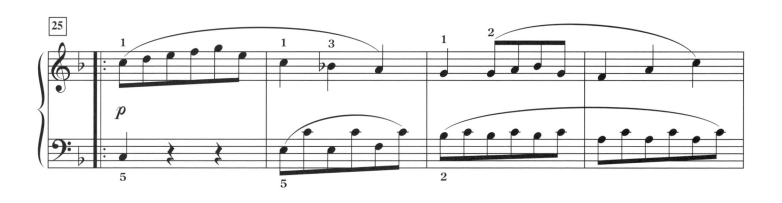

Franz Schubert lived his entire life in Vienna. He composed over 1,000 works and ranks along with the greatest composers of art songs, waltzes and other dances. He died at the young age of 31; very few of his many works were published during his lifetime.

*"I am in the world only for the purpose of composing.
What I feel in my heart, I give to the world."*
Franz Schubert[5]

Minuet in F Major

Franz Schubert (1797–1828)
D. 41, No. 18

[5]Kathleen Kimball et al., eds., *The Music Lover's Quotation Book* (Toronto: Sound and Vision, 1992), 55.

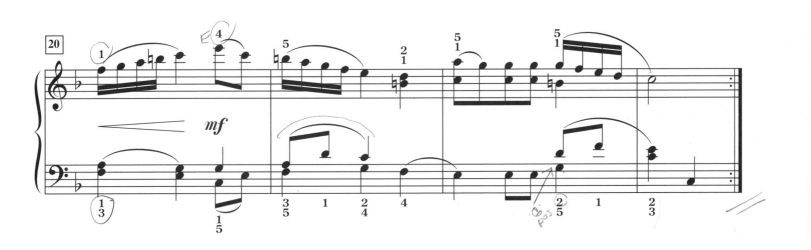

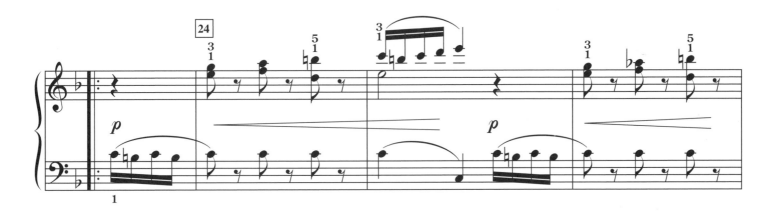

New Romantic Keyboard Effects

Crescendos and Sforzando Accents

As composers expressed more powerful emotions, new keyboard effects developed.
In this **minuet**, notice the:

- crescendos building tension (measures 12, 21–22, 29–30).
- sforzando accents (abbreviated *sf* or *sfz*) (measures 3, 5, 6, 9, 10, 11, 25, 26, 27, 28).
- abrupt changes of keyboard registers (measures 13, 18, 19, 20, 24, 25, 26, 27, 28).
- unusual harmonies (measures 13, 29).
- thicker, fuller textures and sonorities (measures 13–15).

This piece is an example of Beethoven's Classical-Romanticism:

- This is a minuet, a familiar dance during the Classical Period.
- Beethoven has expressed his emotions and feelings, giving the piece deeper meaning. This became typical of Romantic composers.

Minuet in D Major ⓐ

Ludwig van Beethoven (1770–1827)
Wo0 7, No. 7

ⓐ The Minuets from Wo0 7 were originally written for orchestra for a masked ball in Vienna in 1795. A few weeks later they were published in a piano reduction "by the author himself."

ⓑ If it is uncomfortable to reach the entire chord (measures 1, 13, 14, 15), the Editor suggests omitting the notes in parentheses.

Dramatic Crescendos and Keyboard Tremolos

Carl Maria von Weber is another Romantic who introduced new keyboard effects such as dramatic crescendos and keyboard tremolos (measures 9–12).

German Dance

Carl Maria von Weber
(1786–1826)

Glissandos

Louis Köhler, like other Romantic composers, was involved in many aspects of music.

- ▣ He was a composer, pianist, conductor, teacher and writer.

- ▣ His best-known compositions are educational piano pieces written for students.

This piece uses another new Romantic keyboard technique—**a glissando**.

Maybeetle, Fly!

Louis Köhler (1820–1886)
Op. 243, No. 43

ⓐ To play the glissando, after playing the starting note G with finger 2, turn the right hand so the fingernail of finger 3 touches the adjacent A. Sweep the forearm across the keyboard, sliding off the keyboard on the high C. Time the motion to arrive on the high C exactly on beat 1. Depress the damper (right) pedal for the glissando. (Changing to finger 2 on the high C is another way of ending the glissando.)

Beethoven's Piano

As composers like Ludwig van Beethoven expressed more powerful emotions and began using new keyboard effects, they discovered that early 19th-century pianos were not sturdy enough for some of these effects. When Beethoven played, his "fiery expression" broke hammers and strings.

A page turner for Beethoven described it:

> *"I was mostly occupied in wrenching the strings of the pianoforte which snapped, while the hammers stuck among the broken strings. … Back and forth I leaped, jerking out a string, disentangling a hammer, turning a page, and I worked harder than Beethoven."*[6]

Photo: Oberösterreichisches Landesmuseum

1803 Érard (owned by Beethoven and made in Paris, France, now property of the Oberösterriechisches Landesmuseum and can be seen in the Schloßmuseum, Linz, Austria)

- The keyboard length is 5¼ octaves.

- The piano frame is made of wood.

- The string tension is less than two tons.

- The hammers are covered with leather.

[6]Harold Schonberg, *Great Pianists* (New York: Simon and Schuster, 1966), 74.

The Romantic Piano

Pianos significantly changed between 1820 and 1870 as a result of technology that was developed during the Industrial Revolution.

- Iron added to the wooden frames allowed strings to increase in size and tension.

- Stronger frames and strings made it possible to use larger and heavier hammers.

- Heavier strings and hammers made the piano tone richer and more powerful.

- Stronger frames could hold more strings, allowing the keyboard to increase in length.

The Piano Frame: From Wood to Cast Iron

Late 18th century: One iron brace is added to strengthen the wooden frame.

1825: The heavier wooden frame has more iron braces.

1850: Iron bracing adds strength, allowing greater string tension.

1870: The modern frame is all cast iron.

1840 Érard (made in Paris, France)

- The keyboard length is 7¼ octaves.

- The piano frame is now braced with iron.

- The strings are thicker and pulling almost the modern 30-tons pressure.

- The hammers are larger and covered with felt.

The Influence of Literature

Inspiration was essential to Romantics, and many artists were **inspired by literature**. Romantic music frequently takes on a literary role, telling a story in sound. Many 19th-century musicians, such as Robert Schumann (1810–1856) and Franz Liszt (1811–1886), were well-read and socialized with literary and artistic people. They were writers as well as composers.

Born in Hungary, **Stephen Heller** studied in Vienna with Carl Czerny (1791–1857) where he met Ludwig van Beethoven (1770–1827) and Franz Schubert (1797–1828).

- Heller toured as a pianist, and was friends with Schumann, Chopin and Liszt.

- In Paris, he taught piano, wrote music criticism and composed over 160 piano pieces.

Curious Story

Stephen Heller (1813–1888)
Op. 138, No. 9

Molto vivace

ⓐ The Editor suggests that grace notes be played before the beat.

ⓑ See the section "The Pedal in Romantic Music," page 31.

The Ballade

Ballades are a literary form, originating in the Middle Ages.

- They tell a tale in verse.

- Typical subjects are a knight's escapades, a great historical event, love or adventure.

- When composers use the term, the actual story is usually left to the imagination.

- Burgmüller's use of the terms *misterioso* (mysteriously) and *dolce* (sweetly) are clues to his thoughts.

Johann Friedrich Burgmüller was a German pianist and composer who spent time in Paris.

- He was a popular pianist in Parisian salons.

- He is best known for his hundreds of teaching pieces.

Ballade

Johann Friedrich Burgmüller
(1806–1874)
Op. 100, No. 15

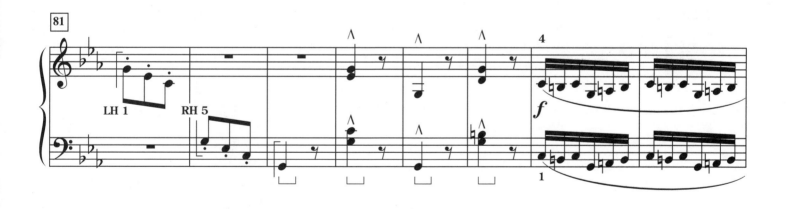

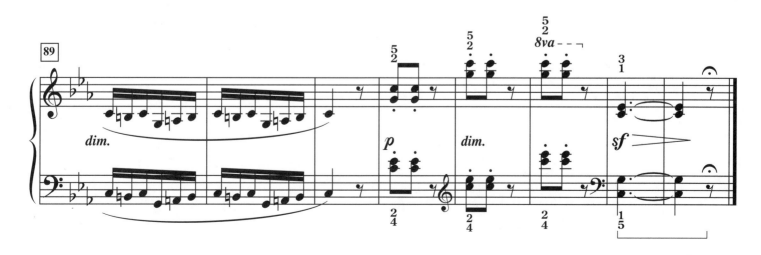

The Influence of Nature

Romantics had an intense, almost mystical **appreciation of nature**. Its variety of moods triggered a wide range of emotions. Artists:

- could find comfort and peace in forests and fields.

- felt helpless against nature's force in a natural disaster.

- idealized nature as representing a world untainted by humans.

A German pianist and composer, **Fritz Spindler** wrote chamber music, symphonies and other large forms, but is best known for his over 300 piano pieces.

Flying Leaf

Fritz Spindler (1817–1905)
Op. 123, No. 10

The Pedal in Romantic Music

"The correct way of using the [damper] pedal remains a study for life."
Frédéric François Chopin (1810–1849)[7]

The right, or damper, pedal has been called the "soul of the piano."
Use this pedal:

- to connect or sustain tones already struck.

- to make a richer tone by allowing strings not struck to vibrate sympathetically.

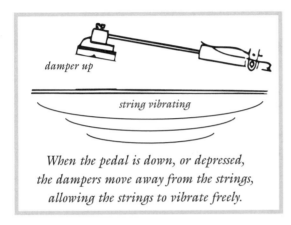

When the pedal is down, or depressed, the dampers move away from the strings, allowing the strings to vibrate freely.

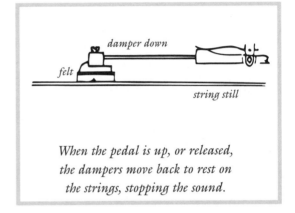

When the pedal is up, or released, the dampers move back to rest on the strings, stopping the sound.

In Classical style music, the damper pedal is used primarily for enriched tone, and is indicated sparingly. It is like "frosting on a cake." In Romantic piano music, the damper pedal is an essential ingredient, and its use is usually assumed, even when not indicated on the printed page.

The most common pedaling in Romantic music is syncopated, legato, or continuous pedal, which maintains the tone color of the dampers being separated from the strings. In this type of pedaling:

- do not blur harmonies, melodic line or phrases.

- change (by quickly depressing and releasing the pedal) immediately after playing a new chord.

- change with perfect "timing," or coordination of the fingers and foot. This requires careful listening, as the ear is the best judge for clarity.

There are several different markings to indicate use of the damper pedal.

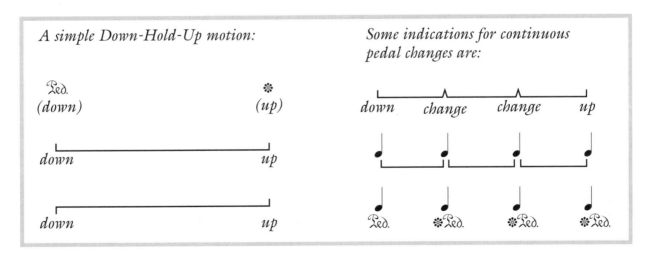

[7]Joseph Banowetz, *The Pianist's Guide to Pedaling*
(Bloomington: Indiana University Press, 1985), 179.

Pedaling Louis Köhler's *Christmas Bells*

Sometimes composers deliberately indicate a **special pedal effect**. In Köhler's *Christmas Bells* changing the pedal only at the beginning of the measure blurs some treble harmonies, but adds to the effect of ringing church bells.

Christmas Bells

Louis Köhler (1820–1886)
Op. 210, No. 25

Special Pedal Effects

To better project their musical intentions, Romantic composers indicated various uses of the pedals:

- ■ to change tone colors.

- ■ to create atmosphere and mood.

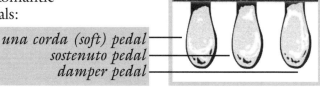

una corda (soft) pedal
sostenuto pedal
damper pedal

Left, Soft or *Una corda* Pedal

When the left pedal is depressed on a grand piano, the entire keyboard shifts slightly to the right, so the hammers are striking one string (on modern pianos, two strings are struck), rather than two or three. On upright pianos, the hammers are usually moved closer to the strings so they do not have as great a striking distance. Common indications for use of the left or *una corda* pedal are:

- ■ *una corda, u.c.* (Italian for "one string")—depress or push down the left pedal.

- ■ *tre corde, t.c.* (Italian for "three strings")—release or let up the left pedal.

Use of the *una corda* or left pedal:

- ■ causes the piano to make less sound, since not all three strings are being struck.

- ■ changes the quality of sound or tone color, since the string(s) not being struck vibrate sympathetically with the others.

Using the *una corda* pedal has no effect on the damper pedal, which can be changed freely while the *una corda* is depressed. In the following piece, *How Lovely Is the Forest!*:

- ■ use the *una corda* and damper pedals at the same time (measures 15–16, 18, 20, 28 and 30).

- ■ listen carefully to blend the "echo" with the ringing tones of the previous measure.

- ■ notice the change in sound (rather "dry" tone color) when the damper pedal is not used in measures 21–22 and 31–32.

Waltz-Style Pedaling with the Damper Pedal

(Use this technique with Grandma's Waltz *by Joseph Lanner, pages 46–47.)*

- ■ The bass note, usually on beat 1, is frequently the root of a chord.

- ■ Notes that complete the chord are usually found on beats 2 and 3. The first note of the left hand in a waltz pattern (beat 1) should be connected to the chord (beat 2) by use of the damper pedal.

- ■ To give the graceful "lift" necessary to a waltz, the damper pedal should be released on the third beat of the measure.

First practice the pedaling while saying in rhythm:

Count: 1   2   3
Down   Hold   Up
(Repeat many times. Do not play the left hand yet.)

Next, practice the left hand alone, with pedal.

Pedal while saying:

Down Hold Up   *Down Hold Up*   *Down Hold Up*   *Down Hold Up*
1   2   3   1   2   3   1   2   3   1   2   3

How Lovely Is the Forest!

Louis Köhler (1820–1886)
Op. 243, No. 29

Un poco lento

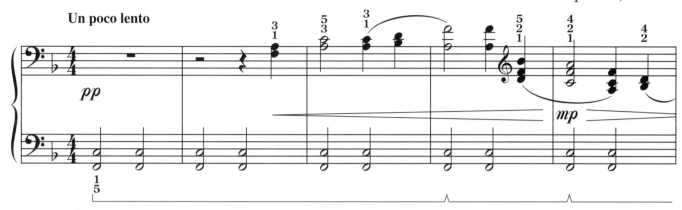

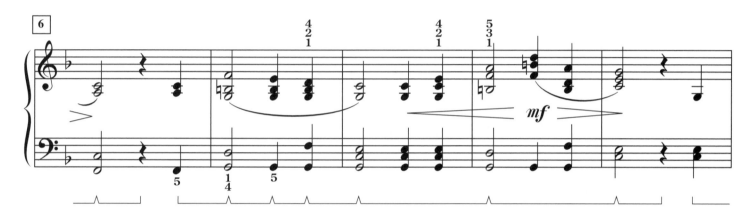

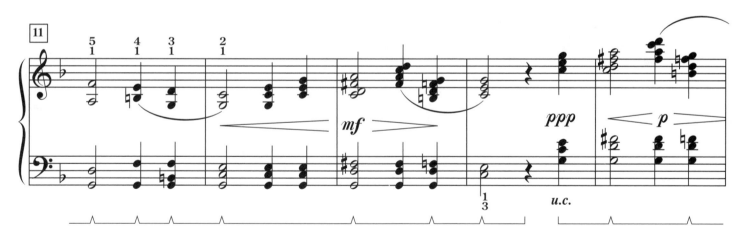

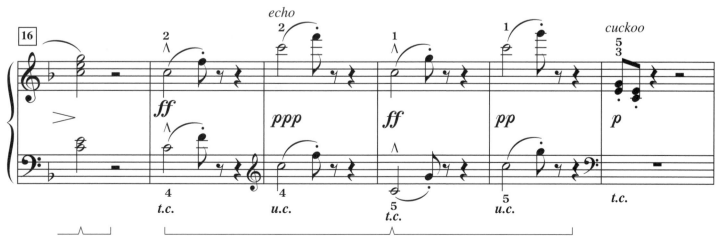

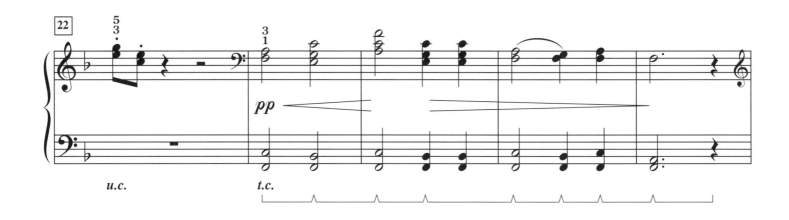

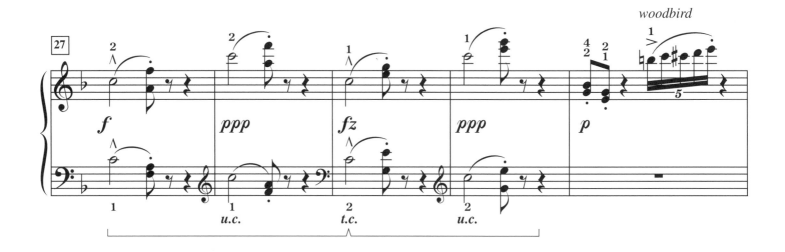

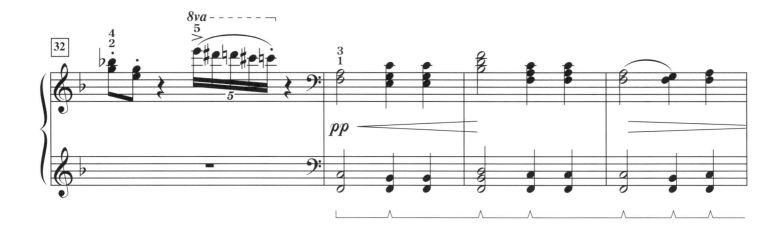

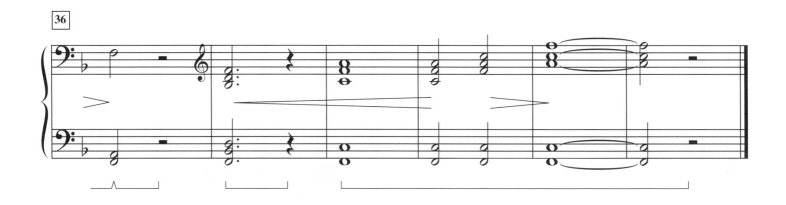

The Damper Pedal and Romantic Sonority

Romantic composers relied on the damper pedal to sustain the bass line, which also enhanced sympathetic vibration, and allowed the piano to "sing."

Romantic composers routinely have the damper pedal hold notes in the lower register while the same hand moves to higher notes. In such places:

- notes in the two ranges are usually a broken chord or tones of the same chord.
- use of the pedal may or may not be marked.
- the damper pedal should be used unless indications suggest not using it.
- listen carefully to ensure that the upper tones blend with the sustained bass tones.

This example is the bass clef of measures 36–47 of the *Prelude,* pages 38–39, by Stephen Heller (1813–1888).

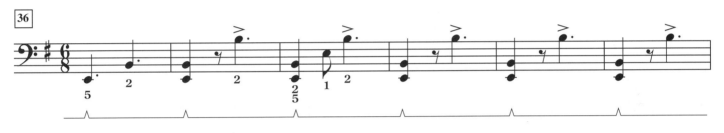

 # The Character Piece

Romantic piano composers, being more concerned with expression than structure, lost interest in the sonata form. They favored the **character piece** which:

- expressed a mood or impression in a short, lyric form.
- was most commonly in **ternary** or **A-B-A** form.
- had a variety of fanciful titles, such as bagatelle, ballade, idyll or prelude.
- although carefully composed, had a feeling of improvisation—a momentary emotion or inspiration expressed in sound.

The Prelude

In the 19th century, a prelude was a type of character piece. Originally a prelude:

- ▣ served as an introduction to another work or group of works.
- ▣ came from the custom of early piano performers who improvised before their programs to get the audience's attention ("preluding").

This **prelude** comes from a set entitled *32 Preludes for Mademoiselle Lili.*

Prelude

Stephen Heller (1813–1888)
Op. 119, No. 6

The Idyll

An **idyll** is a short literary work or piece of music describing a rural or pastoral scene. A pastoral is most commonly about shepherds, their work and way of life.

Cécile Chaminade was a well-known French pianist and composer.

- She performed throughout Europe and in the United States.
- She wrote over 350 compositions, most of which were published during her lifetime.

"This is not a woman composer, this is a composer who is a woman!"
Ambroise Thomas (1811–1896), French opera composer[8]

dyll

Cécile Chaminade (1857–1944)
Op. 126, No. 1

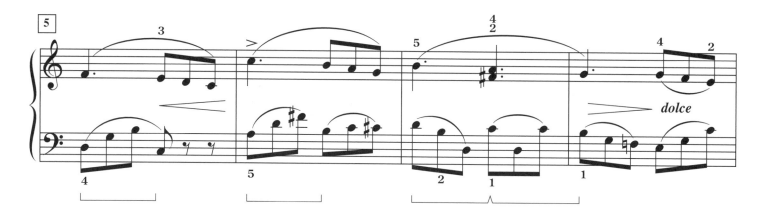

[8]John Jerrould, "Piano Music of Cécile Chaminade," *American Music Teacher* 37 (January 1988): 22.

ⓐ The Editor suggests that grace notes be played before the beat.

Program Music

Program music, which is music associated with a nonmusical event or idea, was developed in the Romantic Period. The event or idea that inspired the piece is indicated in the title or in an explanation of the music.

Sleighing-Party

Louis Köhler (1820–1886)
Op. 243, No. 20

(a) The Editor suggests that grace notes be played before the beat.

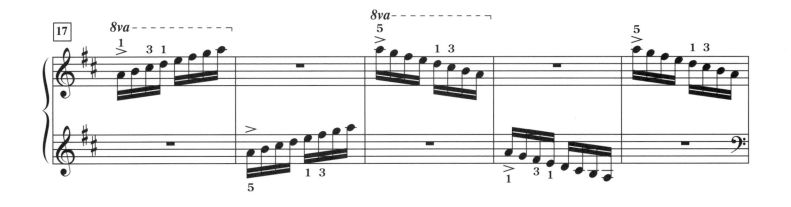

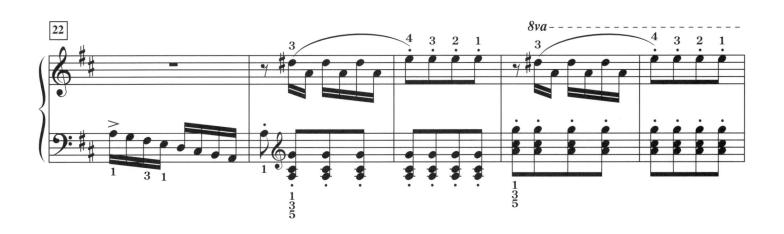

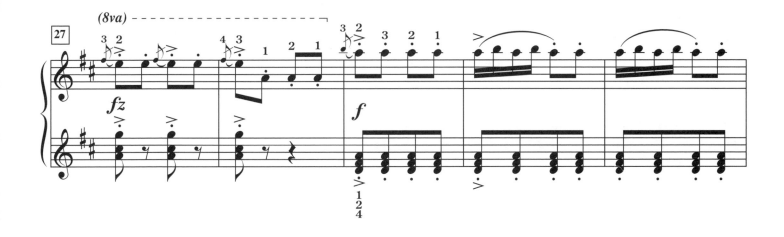

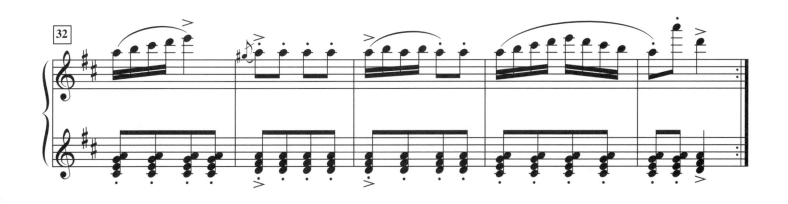

Romantic attraction to the "long ago and far away" created a renewed interest in the Middle Ages, along with its myths, legends and fairy tales. Romantic artists were fascinated with magic and all aspects of the supernatural.

Born in Germany, **Theodor Kullak** studied in Vienna with Carl Czerny (1791–1857).

- He was pianist to the Prussian Court.
- He was a founder of the Berlin Conservatory.
- He composed many piano works, his most famous being his octave studies.

itches' Dance

Theodor Kullak (1818–1882)
Op. 4, No. 2

Allegro animato

The Romantic Dance

The Waltz

The waltz, derived from the German word *wälzen* (to turn or whirl), was one of the most popular ballroom dances in 19th-century Europe. It was the first dance where couples embraced.

The English composer and musical historian Charles Burney (1726–1814) wrote about the waltz in 1805:

> *"How uneasy an English mother would be to see her daughter so familiarly treated, and … the freedom is returned by the female!"*[9]

Dance teachers, quick to come to the waltz's defense wrote:

> *"[It was] a promoter of vigorous health and productive of an hilarity of spirits."*[10]

Vienna is associated with the waltz due to **Joseph Lanner** and Johann Strauss, Sr. (1804–1849). They:

- were string players who performed at coffee houses and restaurants.
- formed an orchestra, which became so much in demand that it was divided.
- each composed hundreds of dances and played as they conducted.

Grandma's Waltz *from The Children's Ball*

Joseph Lanner
(1801–1843)

(a) See the section "Waltz-Style Pedaling with the Damper Pedal," page 34.

[9] *Grove's Dictionary of Music and Musicians,* 5th ed. (1970), s.v. "Waltz" by Andrew Lamb.
[10] Ibid.

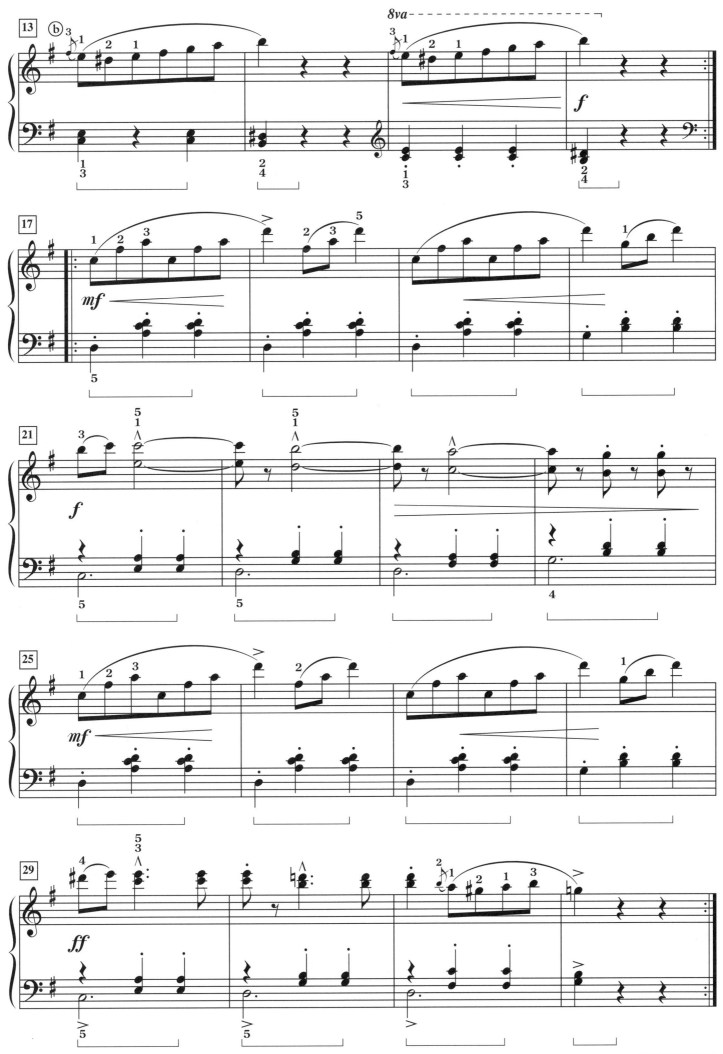

ⓑ The Editor suggests that grace notes be played before the beat.

The Galop

A galop is:

- a very lively round dance.
- danced with hops and gliding steps.

It was popular in 19th-century ballrooms in Europe and at the U.S. White House.

A burlesque is a humorous piece.

Cornelius Gurlitt was a German whose best-known piano pieces are for children.

Galop Burlesque

Cornelius Gurlitt (1820–1901)
Op. 12, No. 6

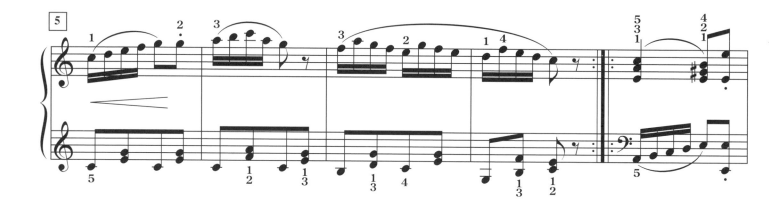

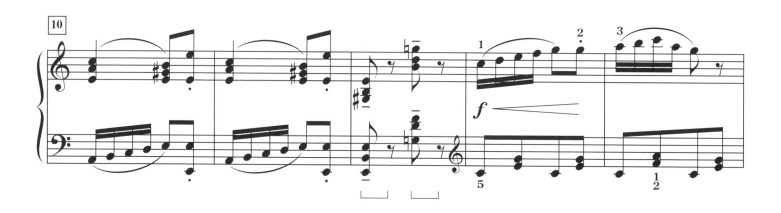

(a) Bottom notes of the octaves may be omitted.

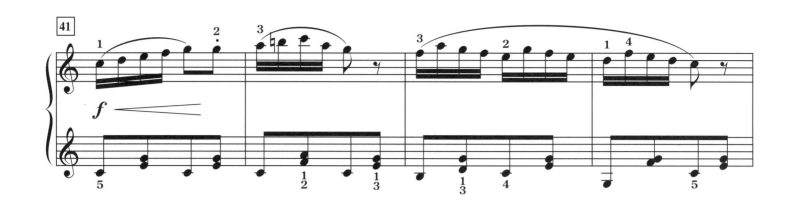

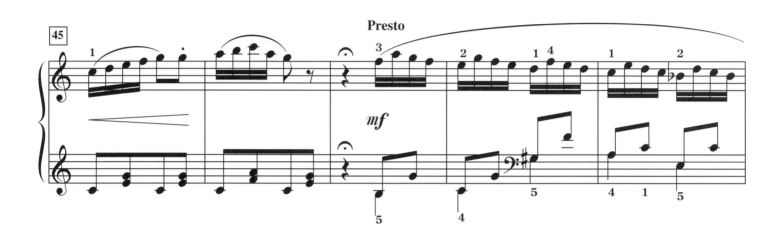

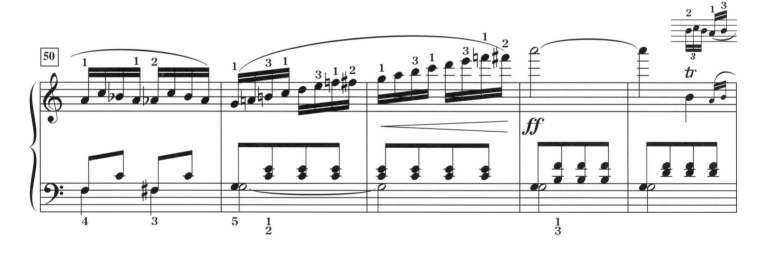

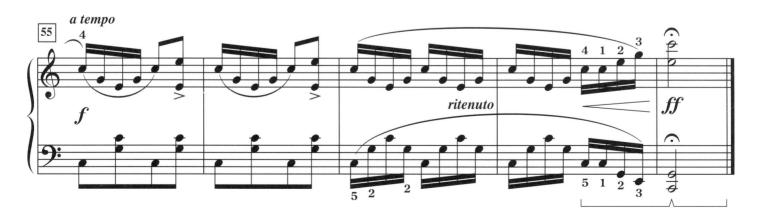

The Piano in the Home

*"Show me the home wherein music dwells,
and I shall show you a happy, peaceful
and contented home."*
Henry Wadsworth Longfellow (1807–1882), American poet[11]

Many middle- and upper-class, 19th-century homes had pianos. At this time, life for most of the women in these families:

- centered around the home.

- was enriched by piano lessons since music was considered to be their ideal outlet.

© Planet Art

The pianist and witty musical scholar Arthur Loesser (1894–1969) observed:

The idleness of his wife and daughters was a necessary feature of a man's prestige as a gentleman. ... It looked more ladylike to do something uselessly pretty than to do nothing. ... Skills in the fine arts (even superficial) were known as "accomplishments."[12]

Unless a family lived in or near a large city, they could never hear operas or symphonies. To make this music more available, music publishers arranged for piano:

- versions of popular operatic melodies.

- symphonies for four-hands.

- folk songs and other popular tunes of the day.

- many of the popular dances of the day.

[11] Craig H. Roell, *The Piano in America: 1890–1940* (Chapel Hill: University of North Carolina Press, 1989), 1.

[12] Arthur Loesser, *Men, Women and Pianos* (New York: Simon and Schuster, 1954), 267.

Lady of the Lake was an exceedingly popular poem by the poet and novelist Sir Walter Scott (1771–1832). It was set:

- in several songs by Franz Schubert (1797–1828).

- as an opera by Gioacchino Rossini (1792–1868), performed throughout Europe and the United States.

- to music by the English composer **James Sanderson**.

In the Sanderson version, a Scottish Highland Chieftain is greeted with a boat song, "Hail to the Chief."

- When performed in New York City in 1812, it became an instant hit.

- "Hail to the Chief" was first associated with the President of the United States at a July 4th celebration in 1828, and this association remains today.

Hail to the chief, who in triumph advances,
Honor'd and blessed be the evergreen pine! . . .

. . . Row, vassals, row, for the pride of the Highlands!
Stretch to your oars for the evergreen pine![13]

March and Chorus *"Hail to the Chief" from Lady of the Lake*

James Sanderson
(1769–1841)

Bold and stately

(a) The Editor suggests that grace notes begin on the beat.

[13] Elise K. Kirk, *Music at the White House* (Urbana and Chicago: University of Illinois Press, 1986), 45.

Janissary Music

Fashionable in 18th- and 19th-century Europe,
Janissary or Turkish music:

- originated with the Sultan's bodyguards, Turkish soldiers who used drums, cymbals, triangles and tambourines as part of their military music.

- influenced military bands in Poland, Russia, Austria, Prussia and Britain, as they all added Turkish instruments.

- was adopted by European orchestras as they added percussive elements, emphasizing jingling instruments.

- influenced pianists as some pianos had "janissary" pedal attachments.

Janissary Band.

Muzio Clementi, an Italian composer, pianist, conductor, music publisher and piano manufacturer:

- spent most of his musical life in London.

- composed eight waltzes for piano and optional janissary instruments.

Waltz in E-flat Major *for Piano, Triangle and Tambourine*

Muzio Clementi
(1752–1832)